The Horn of Africa

Strategic Magnet in the Seventies

J. BOWYER BELL

PUBLISHED BY
**Crane, Russak &
Company, Inc.**
NEW YORK

National Strategy
Information Center, Inc.

Published in the United States by
Crane, Russak & Company, Inc.
347 Madison Avenue
New York, N.Y. 10017

Copyright © 1973 by
National Strategy Information Center, Inc.
130 East 6th Street
New York, N. Y. 10021

Library Edition: ISBN 0-8448-0255-7

Paperbound Edition: ISBN 0-8448-0256-5

LC 73-89523

Strategy Paper No. 21

Printed in the United States of America

Table of Contents

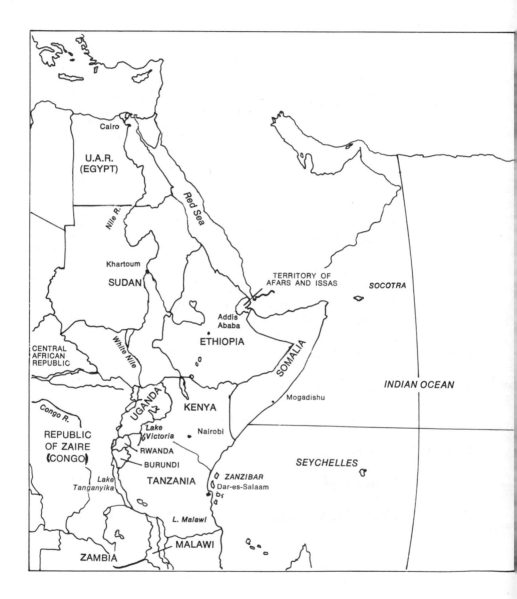

Preface

The Horn of Africa is rarely treated as a significant strategic area in contemporary analyses of United States foreign policy. But in recent years, the region has attracted growing interest because of the obvious geographical importance of its location between Africa and the Middle East, abutting the vital oil routes out of the Arabian Sea, and also because of the developing Soviet naval presence in the Indian Ocean.

Many of the Horn's regional stresses and strains have long historical roots. Coupled with the very serious problems of development, the result is a level of instability that invites great power interest. The United States has long had a communications facility at Asmara, the capital of the Ethiopian province of Eritrea; the French retain their colony at Djibouti, at the southern tip of the Red Sea; and the Russians have cultivated intimate ties with the Somali government. Other powers—in particular, the main protagonists of the Middle East crisis, the Arabs and Israelis—are also profoundly interested in the future of the Horn.

In the present monograph, Dr. J. Bowyer Bell presents a lucid analysis of the present and potential strategic importance of the Horn of Africa. He focuses on internal trends in the Sudan, Ethiopia, and Somalia; the main patterns of regional stress; and the interests of the major powers in the area. The result is a primer of the importance of the Horn for world politics, and a knowledgeable glimpse of what the future may hold for this vital quarter of global politics.

Dr. Bell was educated at Washington and Lee University, and earned his Ph.D. at Duke University. He has taught at Georgia Southern and the New York Institute of Technology, and served as a Research Associate at the Center for International Affairs, Harvard University, and the Center for International Studies, M.I.T. He is now a Research Associate at the Institute for War and Peace Studies, Columbia University. He has written extensively on the main problems of world politics and revolutionary warfare, with special reference to the Middle East and the Horn of Africa.

Frank R. Barnett, *President*
National Strategy Information Center, Inc.

December 1973

1

Introduction

The Horn: A Definition

The Horn of Africa is a vast spearhead stabbing into the Indian Ocean south of the Arabian Peninsula. Politically, the area comprises four states: the Somali Republic along the coast of the Indian Ocean; the French Territory of Afars and Issas—better known as Djibouti—an enclave at the southern end of the Red Sea; the Ethiopian monarchy in the center; and the Sudan at the base of the spearhead stretching deep into the Sahara and north to Egypt. There are few ports—Djibouti, the Somali capital of Mogadishu, and the Ethiopian outlet to the Red Sea at Massawa: and few large cities—Addis Ababa, the Ethiopian capital, Asmara to the north, and Khartoum, capital of the Sudan. The most striking geographical features are the massive Ethiopian highlands, quite unlike any other African area, and the two Niles, the Blue dropping abruptly from the Ethiopian highlands to meet the White Nile twisting slowly north from Central Africa at

1

Khartoum. Much of the rest is low-lying bush, desert, or waste. Scattered across the Horn—a region almost the size of Europe—is a mixed and diverse population, different races, religions, languages, traditions, and attitudes, united only by geography and the consequences of history.

Geography

In the center of the Horn rise the rugged and largely inaccessible highlands of Ethiopia, a maze of flat-top peaks reaching heights of more than 15,000 feet. An isolated land of twisted valleys and ravines, Ethiopia is cut in half by the great Rift Valley. To the west, the mountains taper off into the rain forest and bush of the southern Sudan, a wild and isolated area of great swamps and brush country. The southern reaches of the Sudan may be a potential Eden; but it is now almost untouched except by the tools of primitive, subsistence farmers. Cut by the White Nile that meanders north from Lake Victoria through the great Sudan swamps to meet the Blue Nile slashing down from Lake Tana in the Ethiopian highlands, the Sudan—like Egypt—is a child of the Nile. The Sudanese Niles, however, are very different from those of Egypt. North of Khartoum, where the two meet, the river wanders in great loops through deserts dotted with old ruins and the tracks of camels. In the south and center, the Sudan is lush, watered by the two rivers. The north, on the other hand, is a vast, arid, largely uninhabited waste where the Sahara sweeps past a few oases across to the Red Sea, a land of nomads and dunes, distant emirs and empty space.

The Sudan is huge, nearly the size of Western Europe, embracing some 967,500 square miles. It is ill-served by roads, and dependent on a few rail lines and the Nile for internal communications. Ethiopia, too, is massive. Its area of 471,653 square miles is larger than France and Germany together. Not all of the country consists of the potentially rich highlands, where at some points the topsoil is fifteen feet deep. In the north, beyond the Eritrean highlands, there is a drop to stark wadis and ravines. The terrain east to the Red Sea coast is an equally bleak stretch of barrens, in places below sea level—a land of lava outcrops, salt flats, and temperatures rising to 140°F. The coast of the Horn cuts around the French port at Djibouti, which is the railhead for the track up to the Ethiopian capital at Addis Ababa, and then eastward to the tip of the spearhead at Cape Guardafui. This is the Somali coast, mountains to the north, and low plains along the southern coast, hotter and more fertile, watered by uncertain rivers from the Ethiopian highlands.

The Horn is a mixture—of great beauty and the most barren waste, huge promise and bleak prospects, great rivers and fearful deserts, rugged mountains and endless bush. Basically, it comprises the Ethiopian highlands, overlooking the valleys of the Nile on one side and the Somali coast on the other. The Horn is cut off from the north and west by the Sahara, and in the south and east by the dry bushland of East Africa. There are no great ports, few all-weather roads, and only the beginnings of a railway network (five lines in the Sudan, two in Ethiopia, and none in Somalia). There are local air services to provincial towns; but most of the Horn can be reached only by foot or mule (camel in the lowlands), and not at all in inclement weather. Millions of people live in isolation from any real contact with the capital or the world, untouched by the transistor, cut off by habit and geography from a share in the developing world.

Population

The peoples of the Horn are complex mix of races and languages, overlaid and blended, incorporating isolated remnants from the past and the residue of great invasions.

Somalia. The Somalis, bitterly divided into tribes, are centered along the coast where the political map locates the Democratic Somali Republic. Almost completely nomadic until recently, many tribes still wander over the waterless bush of the eastern Ethiopian province of Ogaden and down almost to Nairobi, the capital of Kenya. There is a logic and a unity to the Somalia. A mixture of Mediterranean and Negroid stocks, speaking a language unrelated to their neighbors, and converted to Islam, they have for centuries pushed toward and been driven from the Ethiopian highlands.

Ethiopia. The Ethiopian highlands, particularly north of the Rift Valley, have long been dominated by a Semitic-speaking people who invaded Africa from South Arabia around 1000 B.C. The Amharas created sophisticated empires long before their conversion to Christianity in the fourth century. Along with the related Tigreans, they repelled the repeated invasions of later immigrants. The various dynasties of the Amharic peoples have dominated Ethiopian history; but even today, in an Ethiopian population of over 25 million, perhaps only 30 percent are Amhara-Tigrean. The largest single group are the Galla, who moved into the Horn 400 years ago and may represent 40 percent of the Ethiopian population. Some speak Amharic, many do not. Many have been converted to Christianity or to Islam, while others are still pagan. There are also vast numbers of other ethnic groups and languages, ranging from recent Arabic-speaking immigrants from South Arabia to the Falasha, followers of an ancient Jewish rite. Ethopia is a melting pot of races, languages, and religions.

Sudan. In the Sudan, the mix is only slightly less rich—572 tribes and 32 major languages—because of the predominance of Islam and Arabic in the north. The Arab tribes, fiercely independent, often rigidly Islamic, have over the centuries raided Black Africa for booty and slaves. The latter have introduced new genes into the Sudanese Arab world, softening the Black-and-Tan division—although that division still exists. In the three southern provinces, there are hundreds of African tribes, speaking their own, often little understood languages or English. Whether pagan or Christian, they share little with the north but the Nile.

Djibouti. The French simply created a port on the coastal waste. The local nomads—Afars and Issas as well as Somalis drifted in and out. Added to them is the whole spectrum of peoples attracted by profit or excitement: Yemenis and Jews, Indians and Amharas.

In all four states, the ethnic balance—like the geography—has engendered serious political problems: between the Somalis and their neighbors, including the French in Djibouti; between the Amhara-Tigrean center and the other peoples of Ethiopia; and between the north and south in the Sudan. Religion, language, and tribe have generated conflicts that have overflowed artificial political frontiers and brought instability to the Horn.

2

Strategic Significance

Economic

The Horn is not only underveloped, but is also unlikely to be the beneficiary of some undiscovered great asset that would transform the unpleasant present into a developed future. No matter what ores and oils may be found, the basis of any progress will be agricultural —and there is nothing more time-consuming and wearing that transforming a subsistence peasant economy into a national asset. The agricultural potential of the Horn is enormous: Ethiopia could feed the continent, Sudan clothe the world—and the Somalis might, perhaps, break even with tropical fruit. To turn this potential into reality is the work of generations. It requires an educational revolution, immense capital investment, and the construction of an entire social-economic infrastructure.

Ethiopia and Somalia are two of the world's poorest countries, and the Sudan is not far behind. Despite the vast changes of the last decade, life for millions is short and harsh. Most of the population continues to lead a marginal existence, and will remain outside the modern world for decades to come. The massive poverty, the isolation of much of the population from the economic and political life of the nation, the uneven pace of development that thwarts justifiable ambitions and creates demonstrable injustice, the interplay of personal ambitions with a restricted potential for reward, all but guarantee a high level of instability. No matter what the agricultural potential, this would be the case even if there were justice, vision, and enthusiasm at the center. The lures of charismatic alternatives, alternative regimes and postures, political shortcuts, or economic fantasies and conceits may in some cases prove irresistible.

What the Horn does not offer is a tempting field for foreign investment; there are simply not the resources to exploit. No major power need long balance the strategic importance of bananas or coffee in any list of priorities. There may be money to be made from Ethiopian copper or Sudanese groundnuts, but the strategic attractions of the Horn do not lie in any present or future economic exploitation.

Ideological

The present decade has offered a declining role for the true believer. The old revolutionary ideologues have aged into technicians. Out of the cauldron of the Chinese Cultural Revolution have come cautious and flexibile old men. Few believe any more in permanent revolution. Whatever the orthodox faith, few regimes are willing to sacrifice unduly for the ideas of their youth. Most have quietly put aside their ideals in the name of policy. The Nixon era has brought an end to ideological crusades in favor of rational detente. All this offers the Horn a respite. It is unlikely that distant ideological battles will be fought out here.

Certainly the pragmatic maneuvers of the great powers, and the shifting of local alliances and alignments, will continue. But the conversion of the pagan and the punishment of the heretic will play a lesser role. This means, for example, that the ideological posture of the regime in the Sudan will have declining significance. Only

Colonel Qaddaffi of Libya still cares about orthodox purity. Thus the "success" of the revolutionary ideal in Somalia may be comforting to the Soviets, but no real ideological threat to the West. At best, ideological shifts and pretensions are marginal in an age without new ideas and in an area with such tiny bands of potential converts. In the Horn, the old ideas of religion are far more important.

Political

Ideological posturing aside, the policies of the regimes of the Horn, whether innovative or arising from historical priorities, might have more strategic impact. Clearly the destruction of an ideological protégé by internal rivals—for example, President Nimeiri's suppression of the Sudanese Communists—must at this stage be tolerated by the great power affected. In fact, such toleration is made easier since it is not really to the advantage of any regime to be long alienated from a natural ally—and Russia is a natural ally of the Arabs. Even an African Sudan must seek some sort of accommodation with Moscow, just as any Khartoum regime must not try Cairo's patience too far.

The potential political problem of the Horn would be a clash of two protégé regimes. But since it is unlikely that any of the states of the Horn could pursue a modern war for more than a brief period, any such conflict would be brief and at worst would attract major power "support" only after the need had safely passed. This means that political factors within the Horn may be divisive and disruptive locally, but are unlikely to produce a great power confrontation. More than anything else, the natural, historic rivalries of the Horn guarantee a diversity of patrons. In the fullness of time, a pro-Chinese Ethiopia might well face a pro-Russian Somalia, but the same old local political issues would be the reason for the alignment.

Geographical

The basic strategic importance of the Horn is not the presence of copper deposits, the fate of democracy, or the future of the Ethiopian monarchy; it is simple geography. The Horn commands the Red Sea and the northwestern Indian Ocean littoral. Whether or not the Suez Canal reopens, the Red Sea route will grow in significance. No matter what new discoveries are made, for the foreseeable future Arabian oil and its conduits will increase in importance. No matter what the returns of detente elsewhere, the prospect of power deployments into the Indian Ocean will continue.

It is true that the Horn may be less important than in the era of Western imperialism, and less so with the Suez Canal closed; but it continues to be important nevertheless. The Horn provides sites for future options more than for present advantages. The Americans already have a radio communications facility at Asmara, in Ethiopia, and the Russians in Mogadishu. In time, such sites could well prove quite important. Technological changes or reawakened ambitions or unexpected turmoil could greatly increase their value. The Indian Ocean is very large, and no intelligent strategist can hope to ignore the potential of the Horn.

3

The Basis of Conflict:
The Horn Before 1960

In many ways, 1960 was a critical year in the Horn. In Ethiopia, there was an unsuccessful coup in Addis Ababa against Emperor Haile Selassie I, and serious opposition to the proposed annexation of federated Eritrea, the former Italian colony attached to Ethiopia by United Nations decision. That same year, Somalia became independent, with claims—based on self-determination and the rights of the nomads—on all three of its neighbors: Djibouti, the Ethiopian Ogaden Province, and much of Kenya to the south. In the Sudan, independent for four years, the ineffectual central government at Khartoum had found no solution to regional dissidence in the three southern provinces.

In many ways, these were all very old problems. But a new era had dawned in Africa in the early 1960s—new nations, the departure of the old colonialism, and the arrival of new powers: Russia, the

10

United States, and China. After 1960, the states of the Horn would have to deal with a whole new set of conditions; but the responses would be based on very old historical attitudes.

Ethiopia

The history of Ethiopia stretches far back into the myths and legends of the Queen of Sheba and King Solomon, and to very real alliances with the Byzantine and Portuguese Empires. The splendor of the first great Christian Empire was severely weakened by the attacks of the Falasha—the Ethiopian Jews—and replaced by a new dynasty under King Lalibela. Between 1200 and 1270, the new dynasty carved out of living rock the great monolithic churches that are today Ethiopia's greatest archaeological treasure. The Lalibela dynasty was, in turn, replaced by the Solomonic line, emperors claiming descent from Solomon and Sheba, whose fortunes since then have largely been those of Ethiopia. The present Emperor, Haile Selassie I, Emperor of Ethiopia, King of Kings, Elect of God, and Conquering Lion of Judah, is the latest of the Solomonic dynasty.

During the last 700 years, the Solomonic dynasty has repeatedly faced a variety of challenges. First, there has been the constant incursion of alien immigrants. Again and again, the Christian Amharas—isolated on their mountain tops, cut off from alliance and for centuries even from contact with Christian Europe—met the thrust of new invasions. The greatest threat evolved out of the spread of Islam. The jihad launched by Ahmed Gran in 1527, supported by the Turks in Arabia and strengthened by Somali converts, expanded into the Ethiopian highlands against declining resistance. By 1540, the plight of the Amharas was desperate. Reputedly 90 percent of the population had converted to Islam, and the area remaining under Christian control was small. Only the arrival of a Portuguese expedition at Massawa and the death of Gran in 1543 saved the Empire.

The influx of pagan Gallas, a nomadic people from the south who lapped over much of the Horn, converting to Islam or Christianity and gradually taking to the land, has posed an even greater threat. After 400 years, the process of assimilating the Galla is still

far from complete. And during those four centuries, there were other
alien invasions to cope with as well. As late as 1889, the fanatical
Sudanese Mahdist sect cost the life of Emperor Yohannes IV, who
fell in battle at Metemma.

Simultaneously a new, if not unexpected, threat emerged. The
Europeans returned to the Horn. In 1869, the Italians appeared on
the Red Sea coast and began to move into the Eritrean highlands.
The Empire was only saved by an Ethiopian victory at Adowa. The
British annexed Aden in South Arabia across the Red Sea, moved
into the Somali coast and Kenya to the south. On the west, the
British also replaced the Mahdists in the Sudan. In 1855, the French
bought the coral island that was to become Djibouti. By the last
decade of the century, Ethiopia once more had become an island
under siege—this time surrounded by European imperialists.

Despite the Emperor's efforts at modernization, the Empire proved
no match for Italian troops, and in 1936 was "absorbed" into the
Italian East African Empire. The brief Italian occupation was followed by that of the British, which in the Ogaden lasted until 1947,
five years after the Italian defeat in the Horn, and in Eritrea until
1952, when with United Nations permission Ethiopia absorbed the
former Italian colony. The maneuvers of the Europeans simply un-
derlined the lessons of the past—that the Empire was isolated, under
threat from without, able to depend on no natural ally. The view
from the highlands had changed little since the time of Lalibela.

A second continuing process over the past 700 years has been
the absorption of many alien immigrants into the Empire, their
conversion to Christianity and hopefully to the use of Amharic. The
core of the state has been the Amhara-Tigrean people, their Church
and their Emperor. Yet this core is at best only 30 percent of the
population—and there are within the establishment considerable
internal differences. Outside the core, perhaps somewhat over half
the population understand some Amharic, and perhaps somewhat
under half may be Christian. Ethiopia is a polyethnic, multireligious,
multilingual conglomerate.

Thus, simultaneous with the external challenges, the Ethiopian center has long been involved in an uncertain and unfinished process of assimilation by conversion. Success has complicated the process, for Ethiopia is now larger than ever before. In 1947, the British returned the vast Ogaden populated mainly by Somali nomads. The acquisition of Eritrea brought in not only the Christian Tigreans but also the peoples of the lowlands and the littoral—more Moslem than pagan, often nomadic tribes dedicated to raids and the life of the *shifta*—the bandit. To prevent the full annexation of Eritrea in 1960, the Eritrea Liberation Front was formed and in September 1961 would begin an armed struggle. Over the next decade, this insurrection would become increasingly associated with revolutionary Arab nationalism—the old Islamic challenge writ new. To the east and south, Somali *shiftas* would raid into the Ogaden in the name of a Greater Somalia. And there have been less visible challenges to the center—the Gojjami Amhara, for example, refused to pay the land tax, as did the Moslem Galla of Bale Province.

In the midst of development politics, the center feels challenged. Each threat awakens old memories and presents new dangers. The lowland enemies, possessed of alternate ideologies and languages, may subvert the Empire's uncertain core. To protect the center, all aid like that of the Portuguese against Gran or the British against the Italians can be sought; but none can be trusted. The *ferenji*—the white foreigner—has too often come as an ally and subverted the faith or the state.

But despite the bitter heritage of the past, Emperor Haile Selassie has moved toward the future, not as fast as the radicals would like, far too quickly for the conservatives. Assuming power as Regent in 1916, he "controlled" a fragmented, medieval collection of feudal landlords, jealous barons, and illiterate priests, and an ignorant and divided people. His first task was simply to strengthen the center, weakened by a decade of dynastic disputes. By the time of his coronation in 1930, this had largely been accomplished. Some steps had also been taken to modernize the country and to find acceptance in the international community: membership in the League of Nations, the formal end of slavery, a few new schools, regular contact with the outside world. But little had really changed. The Italian invasion in 1935 brought a considerable investment to the country, particularly in roads; but the Fascist center never really controlled the countryside. The British—who for some time ruled more as an occupier than a friend—offered Ethiopia an example of effective administration. Thus the 1935-47 interregnum, however humiliating, left physical improvements and administrative habits of great use to the Emperor.

Again in control after World War II, the Emperor's goal was to modernize fast enough to meet rising expectations, particularly those of the new Western-trained elite, but not so rapidly as to lose the traditional support of the people or destroy those institutions that had so long defended the monarchy. No one was satisfied, of course; but except for the confused and unsuccessful coup in 1960, opposition remained muted. Beyond his borders, the Emperor sought to win as many friends as possible, attract as many investors, visit as many states, welcome as many dignitaries. Most of all, Ethiopia needed a committed great power as an ally, ideally an ally with mutual interests and limited African ambitions. The revolutionary regime in Russia was a natural ideological enemy; the old imperialists—Britain, France, and Italy—fading in strength and proven enemies; the small powers—Sweden or Israel—too small. So Ethiopia turned to America; for if no *ferenji* is wholly satisfactory, the American connection was the best option. In 1953, Ethiopia and America signed a Mutual Defense Agreement and an accord that permitted the establishment of a United States communications center in Eritrea. Without becoming a puppet or even a protégé, or cutting his ties elsewhere, the Emperor had forged a great power connection.

The Sudan

In the Sudan, the heritage of history is less heavy, despite millenia of settlement and civilization in Nubia in the north, and down to the edge of the southern forest and swamps. Modern Sudanese history begins with the arrival of Islam in the 15th century. The continual expansion of the faith, particularly into the south, has been a consistent strand of Sudanese history. Conservative and devout, the Sudanese proved sufficiently strong to repulse even the British. In 1885, the followers of the Madhi—the expected Messiah

—stormed Khartoum and killed General Gordon. The independent Madhist state lasted for a decade and the Mahdist Ansar sect continued to be a significant Sudanese power thereafter. Sudanese dedication to Islam had an effect not only on the Europeans, but on the Ethiopian Empire and the African tribes to the south. The former lost an emperor resisting their advance, and the latter's isolation proved no defense against the Sudanese drive for converts and slaves. Until long after 1960, the Ansar remained a crucial element in internal Sudanese politics.

Another important factor in the modern Sudan has been the significance of the Nile—first, as a British imperial interest during the Anglo-Egyptian condominium between 1899 and 1956; and then, more briefly, of vital concern to the Egyptians after Sudanese independence in 1956. The rapid decline of the geopolitical concept of the unity of the Nile has attracted almost no notice. The British went in a rush, and the Egyptians—long preoccupied with the problem of control of the upper Nile—appeared to have more pressing interests. Even without overt Egyptian control of the upper Nile, Cairo assumed that Sudanese friendship and limited Sudanese resources guaranteed that no serious attempt would be made to affect the Nile's course. For the Sudanese, long ambivalent toward Egypt, whose patronizing citizens had little time for "Africans" from the south, there was a strong desire for a connection that would not lash the regime to Cairo's mast. With the decline of Egyptian interest in the unity of the Nile, Khartoum could pursue a more independent policy, although events in Cairo were still closely and often enthusiastically watched.

After the independence of the new Sudanese nation in 1956, the old problems appeared anew. Rebellion in the south, a reaction against historic northern domination, sputtered on. There was constant maneuvering between the forces of the Ansar and their rivals, and a revival of Islam in the Moslem Brotherhood. The Sudan also had the largest Communist Party in the Arab world. The new revolution was fashioned into conservative Sudanese terms, but it was still a threat to the comfortable. Most of all, there was drift. Economic development came slowly. The Sudan continued to depend overmuch on the huge Gezira cotton irrigation scheme, where two

million citizens lived on 64,000 square miles of land around the
fields that produce the Sudan's one great export crop. The Gezira
Scheme, established in 1925, was expanded; but even by 1960, it
was becoming clear that the politicians in Khartoum had few answers
even to the most pressing economic problems. Most intractable of all
was the south, a region untouched by development and unabsorbed
into a Sudan largely Islamic and Arabic.

Djibouti and Somalia

In 1885, the French secured a coaling station on a bleak coral
island at the end of the Gulf of Aden, some 50 miles southwest of
the Strait of Bab el-Mandeb, where the Red Sea meets the Indian
Ocean. This deal with local Issa chiefs, coupled with an arrangement
with the Afars, gave France *La Côte des Somalis* as a counterweight
to British Aden across the Red Sea. Djibouti, built on the coral
island, also became a thin wedge into the Ethiopian highlands. Thus,
while the Italians were being defeated at Adowa in 1896, the French
were able to begin construction of a railway into Ethiopia. Hopefully,
the railway was to reach French Africa at Oubangi-Chari. By 1917,
the railway did reach Addis Ababa; but it went no further. Djibouti
thus became Ethiopia's one window on the outside world until the
absorption of Eritrea in 1952. Between the Italian occupation and
the British presence, Ethiopia could do little about the future of
Djibouti in the postwar period. In 1958, the territory voted three to
one to remain French.

Two years later, on July 1, 1960, former Italian and British
Somaliland were united to form the independent Somali Republic.
The new regime had only the most limited resources, few trained
leaders, a divided colonial heritage, and a history of wrangling tribes
who wandered far beyond the ill-marked boundaries of the new
republic. A central government had to be created, control maintained
over the tribes, and a beginning made on economic development.
With the exception of bananas, largely grown by the Italians in large
plantations, and the export of livestock, agriculture was largely at
subsistence levels; and manufacturing was nonexistent. There was
almost no infrastructure on which to build—few schools, fewer roads,

small and scruffy towns. Subject to both droughts and floods in its one fertile area, the new republic had few charms and no real prospects.

The awesome problems of developing a poor strip of Indian Ocean littoral would have been sufficient challenge for most new regimes. The government in Mogadishu, however, faced what they felt was a unique problem in Africa—much of the Somali population remained outside the country in Ethiopia, Kenya, and French Somaliland. To be sure, colonial borders artificially divided tribes elsewhere in Africa; but in the Horn, Mogadishu insisted that they divided a nation. Based on the principle of self-determination, the Somalis pursued from the first an irredentist policy that challenged the French, the Ethiopians, and the British in Kenya.

4

Internal Instability

There are basically four categories of factors in the Horn that have produced either instability or regional conflict, or both. The first is internal for each state and mainly concerns the pace and pattern of development. Historical problems aside, all of the Horn countries face similar development challenges with limited resources. How well these challenges have been met in part determines relations in the area as a whole, the capacity to accommodate or oppose, the posture of the existing regime. A second factor, more closely related to the historic bases of conflict, has been the interstate disagreements that have led to severe stress, undeclared war, and the export of rebellion. Third, the Horn is not isolated at the edge of Africa and the Middle East, but very much involved in the larger problems of the bordering states. Somali ambitions overlap into Kenya, and the Sudan has close ties with the Arab world. Finally, there are those transnational factors, ideas and faiths that know no boundaries and in one form or another have swept across the Horn, some time in the service of no one in particular, at others tied to special interests.

Ethiopia

Change, at least in urban areas, has been a constant in contemporary Ethiopian society. At the end of World War I, Addis Ababa was little more than a clutch of native villages joined by dirt roads with only the railway station and a few Italianate stucco buildings as a touch of the outside world. Even in 1960, despite a rapidly growing population and considerable building, the Ethiopian capital left much to be desired. By the 1970s, Addis had become a growing urban center of skyscrapers, with an international airport, the ubiquitous Hilton, garden suburbs, and paved roads. Much remained to be done. In and around those skyscrapers are the same old miserable villages crammed with new immigrants from the country. On the countryside, 90 percent of the population continues to live little differently from their ancestors—isolated, often days by mule to the nearest market, without hope of medical treatment or education or a better life. Ethiopia remains terribly poor: at least 90 percent of the population is illiterate; diseases from smallpox to anthrax are endemic and largely untreated outside the urban clinics. Even the most optimistic recognize that future progress will be dishearteningly slow.

A prime concern of the regime has been the development of the country, a process complicated by Ethiopia's isolation, lack of trained manpower, inadequate investment, and the splintered and conservative rural society. Perhaps the first and most basic requirement of development politics is a stable regime. In large measure, the Emperor has provided this; only the failed 1960 coup has stirred the still waters. Many of the new elite feel the waters have been too still, that the Emperor could have moved faster and further, that the old institutions—the Coptic Church and feudal landholdings—need radical surgery. Most, however, are content to wait his passing; for despite some rumors to the contrary, the Lion of Judah is mortal. Consequently, a most pressing topic concerns what will happen to an Ethiopia without the Emperor. Most people feel that whether there is a normal succession—the Emperor buried and the Crown Prince accepted—or some form of military intervention, the next regime will face more difficult problems of stability even if, or especially if, modernization is pressed. Whatever occurs, there is no doubt that the Emperor has in his lifetime transformed a miserable feudal kingdom beyond all recognition.

Beyond the very real and rapid domestic changes—the new roads, the domestic air net, the growing school population—Haile Selassie has had to protect Ethiopia from both internal subversion and external threat. The American connection was the most important step taken in this respect, but close ties were also forged with a number of other countries. Perhaps the most intimate were with Israel; after all, the Emperor descends from the union of Sheba and Solomon; and—more to the point—both have Islamic Arab enemies. Another impressive accomplishment has been to make Addis Ababa the host of Africa and the dream of a united continent. The headquarters of the Organization of African Unity is in Addis Ababa, as is the important United Nations Economic Council for Africa. The Emperor, even to many revolutionary Africans, remains a symbol of opposition to imperialism. Addis Ababa has become the focus of African unity and the venerable Emperor a spokesman for African aspirations. Rich or poor, conservative or not, Ethiopia has an honored place on the African stage; and, because of the Emperor's presence, a significant voice in the world at large.

But despite a willingness to contribute to international projects—Ethiopia sent troops to Korea and the Congo, regularly hosts conferences, and the Emperor has played a personal role in conciliating various African disputes—Ethiopia, like most African countries, has little real power to force events. Many Ethiopians feel that the nation has too little power even to defend its vital interests. The prestige of the OAU is splendid, and within it the Emperor has even managed to win a victory over Somali ambitions. But for many, the old historical threats remain. To counter these, Ethiopia needs more than the moral backing of an independent Africa—and who knows what the *ferenji* ally will do tomorrow.

Sudan

If the 1960s revealed a slow but consistent progress in Ethiopia, the reverse often seemed the case in the Sudan. Faltering and often incompetent political leadership led to a military coup. The new men proved no more capable, and Khartoum witnessed the novel spectacle of a civilian countercoup that deposed the officers. The traditional political leadership wrangled and dithered. The halting pace of development and the constant drain of the insurrection in the south created an atmosphere of quiet despair by the end of the decade. To no one's surprise, there was another military coup in 1969 by Nimeiri and a group of radical young officers. Determined to break with the past and change the future, the new President brought into the regime a number of Communists and radicals who had not been tainted by power and who, despite their revolutionary ideas, remained Sudanese to the core. The new men wanted to transform the old, conservative, static society with radical measures, to find a solution to the perennial southern problem, and to achieve a new united Arab republic.

The obvious model was Nasser's Egypt. Khartoum had always been deeply interested in the Arab world to the north—in the charms of union, the adventures of Nasser, and always the problem of Palestine. The debacle of the Arab defeat in 1967, the erosion of Nasser's reputation, and the difficulties of fashioning an "Arab" solution to the rebellion in the southern Sudan led some of the more radical leaders in Khartoum to consider the alternative of an African future. The key to that future, however, lay in finding solutions to both the southern problem and the aspiration for a new united Arab republic. It was not at first clear that the two goals were mutually exclusive. What was clear to all was that the time had come for radical domestic programs to speed development and root out corruption.

Between 1969 and 1971, the Sudan adopted a radical program and a revolutionary posture. It welcomed the East and criticized the West. There were 500 Russian advisors and SA-2 missiles at Port Sudan. Nationalization laws were passed, the old parties and politicians banned, and the power of the Ansar broken. Yet the insurrection in the south continued and the promise of Arab unity began to dim. Even more depressing, the revolutionary programs proved increasingly unproductive, and the new Eastern friends no less imperialistic than the old Western enemies.

In 1971, Nimeiri reacted to an attempted coup led by Communist officers by reversing the direction of his regime. The Sudanese Communist Party was crushed and relations with the East decayed. Friends in the West and among conservative Arab states were sought anew. The greatest change came in the south. Serious negotiations with the rebels were opened in Addis Ababa in November 1971. The Sudan gave up the dream of a united Arab republic for an accommodation with the southern rebels. Under the auspices of the Ethiopian Emperor, a satisfactory agreement was signed in March 1972 ending over 15 years of insurgency. A Sudanese-Ethiopian detente—long prevented by Khartoum's occasional support of the rebellion in Eritrea and the running sore of the southern Sudanese war—climaxed with a formal border agreement in July 1972. Nimeiri had become a good African, and he turned his nation from the old habits to find a new destiny.

All the old historic currents in the Sudan were deflected. No one cared any longer about the unity of the Nile. The Egyptians had too many problems of their own. The old goal of Arab unity faded before the horror of Colonel Qaddaffi. Even the impulse to conquest of the infidel could not stay the new African course. The Ansar, followers of the Mahdi, were crushed after a bungled attempt at rebellion. None of these seemed particularly relevant to the problems of the Democratic Republic of the Sudan in the 1970s. What did appear to matter was the challenge of creating a viable state whose territory overlapped Black Africa and Arab Africa, Islam and Christianity, desert and jungle—in short, a state seemingly on the margin of all African worlds without membership in any. And for the first time since independence, the Sudan had an almost unchallenged regime, avowedly pragmatic, pursuing a good neighbor policy, and determined on development. Most important of all, the southern problem had become administrative rather than military. Yet, as elsewhere in the Third World, the core was small and fragile, regional instability endemic, and the problems of nation-building vast.

Somalia

The course of events during the 1960s on the other side of the

Horn in many ways reflected the Sudanese experience: an ineffectual center, halting development, and the drain of an insoluble regional problem.

From the beginning, Somalia pursued an irrendentist policy. Even after the OAU refused to support its claim, and without significant allies or an effective army, Mogadishu was determined on the adventure. This was at a time when even the slow pace of development came to a halt. Between 1961 and 1964, famine was averted only by the shipment of relief supplies from abroad, particularly the United States. Opposed by the Kenyans, Ethiopians, and French, Mogadishu simply could not fight a conventional war against superior opponents. The Russians, increasingly interested in the area, came to Somalia's aid with $35 million in 1963. The border "war" waxed and waned. Propaganda brought no converts and diplomacy no fruits. Many of the exiled Somali tribes refused to cooperate. The regime was pursuing a lonely course that endangered the stability of the Horn and the economic future of the Somali Republic.

Eventually the military campaign trailed off. In June 1967, the closure of the Suez Canal devastated the already feeble Somali economy. The one great export crop—bananas—suffered a 60 percent decline in sales to Western Europe in the first year after the June War. Mogadishu drew back. In July 1968, Prime Minister Mohammude Ibrahim Egal took power determined to reach a detente with Ethiopia so that Somalia could get on with development politics. His efforts succeeded in September 1968, and his policy was ratified by Somali voters in the parliamentary elections of March 1969.

Then, in October, President Abdirashid Ali Shermarke was assassinated; and the army, backed by the police, deposed Egal and established a revolutionary regime. For the time being, there was no talk of a Greater Somalia, but only of internal development. The new Revolutionary Council sought to accelerate development by adopting a wide variety of programs, self-help plans, and nationalistic alternatives; the banana plantations, for example, were taken over. Increasingly, the regime depended upon the Soviets, long a major source of aid. Between 1961 and 1972, the USSR extended extensive economic grants and credits, aiding in the construction of schools, printing plants, a radio station, a fish cannery, two hospitals, a milk processing plant, a meat packing plant, and the modernization of the port of Berbera. Despite foreign aid from other nations, including large loans and grants from Italy and several American projects, without Soviet aid the Somali picture would have been bleak indeed.

The new Revolutionary Council felt sufficiently confident in May 1973 to attempt to place their claims against Ethiopia on the OAU agenda. After long and acrimonious debate, the issue was excluded from the agenda by one vote. But the concern of a Greater Somalia was once again alive and well.

Djibouti

The advent of an independent, expansionist Somalia coupled with a general European withdrawal from Africa posed serious problems for the future of Djibouti. At the time of President DeGaulle's visit in August 1966, there were serious riots sparked by the Somalis. In Addis Ababa, the Emperor pointed out that "Djibouti indisputably is ours and its people know they belong to Ethiopia." The French organized another referendum, in which far fewer Somalis were present to vote. The tiny enclave was transformed into the French Territory of Afars and Issas. The Ethiopians were satisfied; and, of course, the Somalis were not. But only a shift in the French presence, probably unlikely in the immediate future after the Gaullist parliamentary success in 1973, might transform the fate of Djibouti into a regional issue.

5

Regional Conflict

Within the Horn

Somali Irredentism. The manuevers of the Somalis at the OAU meeting in Addis Ababa in May 1973 reawakened Ethiopian fears. The Somali claims on the Ogaden have been regarded in Addis Ababa as a mortal threat to the stability of the Empire. Ethiopia as a pluralistic state simply cannot accept the legitimacy of ethnic separatism—a concession that could lead to further demands and ultimate fragmentation. In response to the Somali challenge, Ethiopian experts have pointed out that the Mogadishu regime is a successor state to no historical "empire." There never was a Somalia before 1960, and the quarrelsome and suspicious Somali tribes have always found more grounds for disagreement than reasons to unite. For Ethiopians, the concept of a Greater Somalia is an intellectual conceit, lacking in reality and opposed to the general African agreement that the old colonial boundaries should be preserved lest chaos follow attempted readjustments. In Addis Ababa, there is no complacency about the Somali threat.

The success of the new Revolutionary Council in Mogadishu, limited though it may seem to outside observers in "revolutionizing" the country, has been ominous to the Ethiopians. The new regime appears to be putting its house in order before launching the next round of the struggle—and this time the Somalis will be backed by the Soviet Union. Given the woeful poverty of Somalia and the paucity of its resources, the tiny pool of skilled talent, the continued tribal rivalries, and the state of the army, Mogadishu's aspirations simply do not appear to most observers to be a lethal threat to Ethiopia. The Somalis do have 150 Soviet T-34 medium tanks; but only 30 of these are serviceable, and even these are unlikely to run very long or far in combat conditions. But to Ethiopia, the Somali threat is very real. Each Soviet shipment of arms, each new revolutionary project, creates ripples of anxiety in Addis Ababa. The old Ethiopian establishment fears both the ancient Islamic threat and the new revolutionary doctrine, while the new elite sees rapid social and economic development in contrast to the Empire's more leisurely place; and the army fears the new Soviet weapons.

Unhappily, there is little the Somalis can do to ease the tension. The drive for modernization can hardly be postponed for Ethiopian convenience, and no regime wants a shoddy army when a friendly power will help. More important, no Somali can abandon the dream of a single state incorporating all Somalis. Even in the unlikely event that the Somali leadership publicly did so, no Ethiopian would believe them. The tension might be eased by a long period of detente; but Ethiopian fears are centuries old, and Somali claims are widely held to be just. Both countries feel the necessity to maintain military forces beyond what might otherwise be expected. Hence, conflicting aspirations in the Ogaden could once more lead to conflict, and the possible involvement of distant patrons.

Djibouti's Future. It is difficult to separate the problem of Djibouti from Somali irredentism, except that here Ethiopia does have ambitions beyond the status quo. The Emperor has claimed that "Djibouti indisputably is ours." The Ethiopian case is historically weak and ethnically uncertain. Before France, no one really occupied this arid patch of waste. The Afars, Issas, and Somalis and their camels only passed through. The French colonial name, *Côte des Somalis*, gave Mogadishu only as firm a claim as the number of Somalis in the enclave. Mogadishu suspects that the three-to-one victory for France in 1958 was manipulated, and is certain that the March 1967 referendum creating the French Territory of Afars and Issas (no mention of Somalis) was an exercise in imperialism. There was, however, little that Mogadishu could do; and Ethiopia, long on cordial terms with the French, viewed the results with equanamity. When a pro-Mogadishu Front for Liberation of the Somali Coast appeared, Ethiopia countered with its own Djibouti Liberation Movement. The OAU calmly recognized both as "true" liberation movements, and there the matter has largely rested. Ethiopia and France are content, the Somalis sullen but helpless.

The truly great danger would be a sudden and unexpected French withdrawal—perhaps as a result of a change in government, and hence of colonial philosophy, in Paris. Given the nature of the Ethiopians and Somalis, few would have much confidence in an independent Djibouti devoid of French support. And few in Addis Ababa would tolerate Somali annexation. Djibouti is crucial to Ethiopia because of the railroad; a hostile power in the enclave could cut off the Empire from the Indian Ocean. At the moment, French possession is everyone's second choice, complacently in Addis, reluctantly in Mogadishu; but sudden change would almost certainly open the door to an Ethiopian descent on the enclave, and perhaps a Somali response. In point of fact, the French imperial presence is as much an exercise in peacekeeping as a relic of the colonial past.

The Eritrean Insurrection. While the Somalis were an overt challenge in the past, and may be again in the future, at present the great threat to Ethiopia is the armed struggle waged by the Eritrean Liberation Front. Beginning largely as a response to Ethiopian policy to annex Eritrea, the ELF originally attracted Christians and Moslems, conservatives and radicals—essentially a regional spectrum of separatists who for varying reasons opposed amalgamation with the Empire. The armed struggle, however, did not fare so well. Much of the ELF leadership often remained in exile, and the fighting was done largely by tribesmen who saw little difference between the life of the *shifta*, their historical pursuit, and that of a freedom fighter. The Ethiopians long contended that the "armed struggle" was simply a matter of *shiftas* at home and spokesmen abroad. Nevertheless, the bandits attracted sophisticated aid from abroad, and subverted some members of the elite at home. But the ELF could not seriously threaten the center or even gravely disrupt the province. Under increasing Ethiopian pressure, the ELF began to associate their cause with the Arabs, collecting support from conservative imams for Islamic reasons, and from radical regimes for ideological ones. Much of the Christian population of Eritrea was alienated by the ELF, and few beyond the wild tribes were attracted. Gravely weakened in 1967-68, the ELF revived in 1969-70 only to falter once more in the face of a firm policy of military suppression coupled with the beginning of a pacification-development program.

But despite the difficulties and decline of the ELF after 1971, the insurrection is by no means over. This is true despite the detente with the Sudan, which has closed off what in the past was a haven, and the increasing difficulty in obtaining supplies from across the Red Sea. As long as there are nomadic tribes and *shiftas* willing to be recruited as "freedom fighters," as long as banditry remains a way of life even for the settled population, there will be a potential for disturbance in Eritrea. The investment of relatively little money and arms can cause considerable trouble for the government in Addis Ababa.

Southern Sudanese Separatism. While the Ethiopians have been able to contain their separatist insurrection at relatively little cost, the Sudanese—to the amazement of all—have done even better with the rebellion in southern Sudan. The agreement signed in Addis Ababa in March 1972 ended a sporadic rebellion that began even before Sudanese independence, cost tens of thousands of lives, and distorted the development of the state. Despite dire predictions, Khartoum's conciliation of the insurgents has worked remarkably well. It has not engendered serious resentment in the north, and has reduced the prospect that the Horn might become a battleground between the cultures and peoples of the Arab world and Black

Africa. The accommodation became possible when President Nimeiri turned from preoccupation with Arab unity to the possibility of an African policy, and offered the southerners major concessions. At the same time, the rebels accepted that there would never be sufficient external support to achieve independence.

But the satisfaction of both sides with the agreement, and the ease with which yesterday's guerrillas became today's Sudanese soldiers, does not fully disguise the very real dangers ahead. No matter how enthusiastic both sides, a 20-year war—particularly an irregular war—leaves very serious scars. Moreover, no accommodation will ever quite live up to the hopes of those involved. Finally, and most important, each side has given up a cherished historical posture. The loss of self-determination by the southerners has largely been compensated for by the northern-dominated Sudan's turn toward Africa. Withdrawal from the center of the Arab world, and the problems this may cause, have not been fully recognized in the north. The fate of the Black September guerrillas for example, reawakened old loyalties and greatly complicated Nimeiri's life. The Sudan might now be an African nation, but there was still a good deal of Arab sentiment to consider even when the fedayeen had violated the country's hospitality, murdered old friends, and been manipulated by resentful Arab rivals. The strains of accommodation may be expected, and the evidence is that they will be surmounted. But the potential for schism as a result of personal ambition, errors of policy, and external factors will long exist.

Along the Borders

African Attitudes. Events in the Horn have long attracted the interest of its immediate African neighbors. In one form or another, its problems have lapped over boundary lines—for example, Sudanese refugees in the Congo, or Somali *shiftas* raiding into Kenya. At the same time, there has been an interest in the potential of intra-African institutions and initiatives; after all, the headquarters of the OAU are in Addis Ababa. The potential, however, has seldom been realized. Thus, the OAU's position on Somali claims may actually have aggravated the dispute during the past decade, just as Nimeiri's efforts to play the good African in a recent dispute between Tanzania and Uganda earned him the enmity of Colonel Qaddaffi, who backed Uganda.

One organization that attracted a great deal of interest in the Horn was the East African Community, made up of Kenya, Tanzania, and Uganda. Many of the states of East and Central Africa looked to the East African Community as a possible nucleus for greater regional cooperation. Despite some accomplishment, however, the East African Community by the 1970s faced very real problems. The last straw was the army coup in Uganda led by General Amin, who was anathema in Tanzania and hardly welcomed by Kenya. Amin's ambitions and antics have gone far to destroying not only the Ugandan economy, but also the future of the East African Community. For the states of the Horn, membership in a warring, bankrupt "community" holds little charm. In Ethiopia, Amin's unexpected conversion to anti-Zionism in 1972, his welcome to King Faisal of Saudi Arabia, and his alliance with Colonel Qaddaffi have awakened all the old fears of Islamic encirclement. For the Sudan, now uneasily set on an African policy, a Black African, anti-Zionist, pro-Arab, devoutly Islamic bastion to the south complicates life.

For all the states of the Horn, the charms of East Africa have now gone. Ethiopia and Somalia might someday play a mature and stabilizing role in East Africa, but the reverse no longer appears to be the case.

South Arabia. To the east across the narrow strait of Bab el-Mandeb in South Arabia, there have also been encouraging signs of stability and accommodation during 1972. The long-predicted clash between the Yemen Arab Republic to the north and the People's Democratic Republic of Yemen in the south occurred on schedule. The war, however, produced neither victory nor defeat, nor even a frustrating stalemate, but instead a Unity Pact, initiated in Cairo and signed in Libya. Since the regime in the north at San'a is conservative, supported by Saudi Arabian subsidies, a willing host to exiles from the south, and suspicious of the Marxist-Leninist regime in Aden, many observers doubt that a united republic will emerge in the near future.

The interest of the Aden regime in unity may indicate a decline in revolutionary ardor, and this *would* have a stabilizing effect across the Red Sea in the Horn. In the past, Yemen has been a battleground between East and West, Islam and Revolution, Liberation and Imperialism; but after the Egyptians left the north and Britain the south in 1967, there was hope for a breathing period. The revolutionary new regime in Aden, however, sought to export its ideology and backed revolt in neighboring Oman and Eritrea. Close ties between Aden and Mogadishu also worried the Ethiopians. Addis Ababa responded in a variety of ways, including a threat to expel Yemeni workers from Ethiopia.

Such revolutionary activities created additional tensions in the Red Sea basin. But on the whole, South Arabia has been peripheral to the major concerns of the Horn. What goes on in South Arabia can affect the Horn—as in the case of Eritrea—but hardly determine events.

Arab Neighbors. At one time, Egyptian interests in the Horn were highly important. But since 1967, Cairo has shown much less concern for the area. Few worry about Ethiopian or Ugandan control of the sources of the Nile, or about Sudanese hydrographic intentions. The disastrous Egyptian intervention in Yemen and the June 1967 War—plus Nasser's death—have soured many Egyptians on further adventures. The dream of an Arab republic has narrowed. Egypt has accepted that the Sudan could not take part in the concept and at the same time end the disastrous southern insurrection. For Cairo, a regime in Khartoum not unsympathetic to Egypt's interests, not unaware of the importance of the Nile, and not actively hostile to Arab ambitions, would be acceptable—indeed, would have to do, since Cairo lacked the leverage to force change. And Egypt had little interest in Ethiopia or Somalia. There was some concern about Israeli influence in the Red Sea; but this was really part of the Palestine problem.

But if Egypt has cut its losses to the south and withdrawn, Libya has not. Backed by massive oil resources, Colonel Qaddaffi, emulating Nasser, saw Africa as one more battleground in the Arab-Islamic struggle against Zionism and imperialism. With the aid of the "atheists" in Aden, he aided the Islamic revolutionaries in Eritrea, thereby antagonizing the Ethiopians, whom Libya condemned in the OAU as pro-Zionist. Qaddaffi's assurances and his money convinced General Amin of the wisdom of a pro-Arab, anti-Zionist policy, further alarming the Ethiopians. His growing alienation from Nimeiri complicated the task of government in Khartoum.

In fact, Qaddaffi's swoops and spectaculars tended to make all his neighbors nervous. If the rest of the Arab world did not want to tinker seriously with the stability of the Horn beyond a little aid to the ELF and an occasional harsh word for Nimeiri, this did not seem to be the case with Qaddaffi. And since a little money can buy a good deal of trouble for the fragile and overextended regimes in the Horn, the intentions of Qaddaffi are now a major concern.

Transnational

Islam and Christianity. It seems probable that the new ideas of African unity, haltingly structured in the OAU, will have far less impact than the old, divisive confrontation between Christianity and Islam. Thus, the Ethiopian-Israeli alliance has created additional tension as the Emperor has sought to bring in the Israelis to redress the Moslem imbalance—an ancient confrontation clothed in contemporary strategic clothes. When the Libyans accused Ethiopia of being pro-Zionist and anti-African at an OAU meeting in May 1973, the Ethiopians sensed the ancient threat of Islam, this time backed with vast wealth. Neither Christianity in its various forms nor Islam is simply an idea in the service of this or that regime; both have an independent momentum. The Islamic conversions that so worry the Amharic establishment are individual religious acts that have a cumulative political effect. In the long run, as in the Sudan, there may be an accommodation between the advocates of Islam and Christianity, a moderation of antagonism; but at the moment, the prospect in Ethiopia is for uneasy toleration at best, a toleration that is easily dissipated—as in the case of Eritrea, where the ideas of the 20th century have won far fewer converts for the ELF than the claims of the True Faith.

Hence, Colonel Qaddaffi's actions have awakened old fears, historical loyalties, and neglected aspirations that have long stretched across the Horn. Libyan oil money is often in the service of "anti-Zionism." In Ethiopia and elsewhere, Qaddaffi appears as the new point of an old Islamic lance. As in the past, the Islamic issue is transnational, engendering conflict across boundaries and creating alliances between ill-matched allies. It is not only the Ethiopian establishment that views Islam as an ancient enemy. Many Black Africans elsewhere in the Horn have found themselves for centuries under the threat of forced conversion and/or slavery. Although the Black-and-Tan fault that cuts through Africa between the Islamic-Arabic north and the Christian-pagan-tribal south has always been blurred by intermarriage, conversion, accommodation, and local custom, the confrontation has been real enough, and in the Horn particularly significant because of the energy and capacity of the Ethiopian defense. To the outside eye, the confrontation hardly appears sharp—from Cairo, Khartoum is almost an African city, while from the Congo it is hardly African at all. Indeed, the entire Horn seems marginal, a blend of two worlds swirling about the very special core of the Ethiopian Empire, which with the passage of centuries has become far less special than the core establishment would admit. But in the Horn, the old clash of religions remains a factor.

Revolution and Reaction. Just as the old ideas of the Book still stir the Horn, so too do the new ideas from Moscow or Peking or Cairo. Increasingly in the last generation, the arrival of "revolution," however imperfect the local model, has complicated an already complex array of divisions and antagonisms.

In one form or another, each of the regimes of the Horn from Khartoum to Mogadishu has faced the development problem—and with only limited success. No regime can fulfill the rising expectations of the people or fit quite legitimate priorities into a totally satisfying program. The pace has never been as swift as some of the elite would have preferred. In consequence, any theory of revolutionary development has great appeal, whether it be Arab socialism out of Damascus or Maoist communism parsed from small red books. Both the Sudan and Somalia have sought to impose revolutionary change from the center—expropriation, nationalization, secularism, the importation of radical models. The result has often been divisive, opposed by the conservative bases of society, and has often left the central regime dependent on an uneasy army and its own rhetoric. The usual reaction to the revolutionary path has been an appeal to pragmatism on the ground that the advocates of rapid change know too little of the process and too much about agitation. The practical way is to seek investment from those with funds to invest. This is why Nimeiri turned from the Socialist bloc to the wealthy Arab oil regimes, no matter what their ideology. Thus the alien revolutionary ideologies, however adapted for local use and uniting the likeminded across national boundaries and historical misunderstandings, have also divided those who seek to transform traditional society—and united those who see little need for and much danger in change. No matter how isolated the Horn, the new ideas have complicated life; for Ethiopia, for example, the Somalis are a triple threat—Islamic, irredentist, *and* revolutionary.

This is not to say that the great ideas, particularly of revolution, out of the Western world have had only marginal impact. But once these concepts have arrived in the isolated Horn, they have often been fashioned to adorn old causes or warped to buttress ancient ambitions. Clearly the ideas of Marx and Lenin, and later Mao, have had substantial impact on the educated elite; in the Sudan, the Communist Party became a major political force. Yet a serious obstacle to Marxism in any form has been the persistence of organized religion; the advocates of atheism are rare, indeed, even in the underground ranks of the Sudanese Communist Party. Revolutionaries have thus had to adjust Socialist ideas for local consumption. In Somalia, Marx and Islam have been wedded into the national philosophy of *Iska Wah Ugabso*—self-help that, according to Comrade General President Siad, in no way conflicts with Islam.

The appeals of revolution can be heard across national boundaries. Some radical Ethiopian students support the ELF precisely because it is revolutionary, or at least addresses itself to them in revolutionary terms in violation of all the old historical lessons. If such radicals are few in number, often in exile, and subject to reconversion by maturation, the fact remains that the idea of revolution, even if imperfectly understood, becomes a constant threat to static institutions, a real danger to those who want no change and a goad to those who understand the need for change.

The alternatives offered out of the West—a structured economic development dependent in part on individual capitalist initiative within the context of a democratic government assuring civil rights to the population—have had much less general appeal. The "capitalist" approach, equally imperfectly understood, often appears in a country without capital as a form of neoimperialism. Parliamentary government is another import that has often proved ineffectual and engendered little mass support. The Sudan's two attempts ended in military coups. Ethiopia has the form of a constitutional monarchy, but little of the substance. In Somalia, Egal was displaced by the 1969 coup. There are still those who point out the benefits of Western development strategy, not to mention Western capital, and the importance of civil liberties and democratic political institutions. But they have less impact simply because revolutionary ideas seem to offer a short-cut to economic development and an end to self-serving "political" quarrels. Even when the revolutionary ideas fail in practice, as was the case by 1971 in the Sudan, the young remain susceptible; for after all, Western ideas and policies have also failed in practice.

Inevitably, the sponsors of various ideological alternatives have attracted outside aid and comfort from the ideological source. A revolutionary Nimeiri could turn to the Socialist bloc, while a Haile Selassie could look for assistance from the West. Christian organizations aided the southern Sudanese rebels, just as Islamic groups did in Eritrea. Depending upon the aspirations of the protégé, such aid may add to the stability of the Horn or detract from it. As always, there is a considerable grey area. Do military shipments to Somalia and Ethiopia serve to maintain a precarious balance, or to open the prospect of renewed conflict? Generally, the central world models for the various ideologies have tended to reward conversion—and to accept apostasy. The Soviet move into and out of the Sudan between 1969 and 1971 revealed the limitations of overt intervention from abroad. The Soviets had made and lost a friend, and there was little that Moscow could do but try and save face. The one exception has been the Qaddaffi variant of Islamic-Arabic nationalism; for the Libyan leader can no more tolerate apostasy than welcome atheism. His initiatives may cause more publicity than effective change. But given his resources, his dedication, and his unswerving belief in his cause, the Horn may have to anticipate further well-financed interventions from the north.

6

International Involvements

After an initial fascination with independent Africa, an Africa that engendered great power rivalries, there was a diminution of international interest in the continent. Africa appeared to have made a false start. Democracies disappeared in a flurry of coups; revolutionary leaders discarded all but their rhetoric in a scramble for the comforts of life; unpronounceable tribes slaughtered each other for leftover colonial scraps and for ancient vengeance. The revolutionary powers as well as the Western countries found their new African adventures frustrated by customs older than ideology. The winds of change ceased to blow. White Africa prospered while Black Africa played musical chairs, or so it seemed to the disheartened advocates of the new African dawn. Pragmatically, there was no return on investments in most African countries, limited markets, and little trust in dubious generals and momentary presidents. At first, Russia and the United States had vied over the future of the Congo; the Chinese backed revolutionary movements and agreed to build the Tanzania-Zambia railroad; and elsewhere, old colonial powers remained to manipulate the new regimes. But it soon became clear that the returns were not great for anyone; some mineral wealth could be exploited, and some prestige collected, but little else. Interest slackened, and various powers were left with a residue of not always planned-for African interests.

In the Congo, the Americans had come out ahead due to luck, skill, and the technical capacity to exert force. The Chinese had been left with the railway project in Tanzania, and the Russians with friends in the liberation movements and some entry to a few radical regimes. The French fashioned an effective form of neocolonial control in their old empire. The British did not. The Italians competed for new construction projects with German and Japanese firms. With the possible exception of the French, no one seemed to have an all-African policy. South Africa argued that it fought to protect Western civilization against communism; but Western civilization seemed more interested in the booming South African economy than in the strategic argument.

The Horn, however, could not be left in decent and benign neglect like most of Black Africa, or exploited like the "fortunate" few. The Horn overlapped both the volatile Middle East and the Indian Ocean, abutted imperial lifelines, and flanked the oil-rich states of Arabia. Until the mid-1950s, the Horn mattered to the old imperial powers, and afterward it mattered to those who sought to supplant them. The British and Italians remained in Somaliland until 1960, the French have never left Djibouti, and the Americans made a formal arrangement with Ethiopia in 1953. Then the Russian Navy arrived at Hodeidah across the Red Sea in Yemen, and signed a military agreement with Somalia. There would be Russian advisors in the Sudan, American Peace Corps volunteers in Somalia, Chinese diplomats in Aden. There was to be an Israeli-Arab incident in the Strait of Bab el-Mandeb, and for five years there were tens of thousands of Egyptian troops in Yemen. The Horn thus remained on the edge of major events—a flank that could not be neglected, and where all contenders felt that they had some legitimate interests.

The United States

The United States had few traditional interests in Africa. Not many Americans had heard of Khartoum or Mogadishu. The same was not quite true of Ethiopia; Haile Sclassic's League of Nations speech had left a residue of admiration. There was general support for African independence; but sympathy and admiration hardly formed the basis for an American involvement in the Horn.

To a degree, the subsequent American connection with Ethiopia resulted from an African initiative. The Emperor wanted American support; and Washington, in turn, could see the advantage in Cold War terms of a formal link with an old friend, however small and distant.

Despite the historic suspicion of the *ferenji*, the Ethiopians had sound reasons for seeking an American connection. America was an enemy of Communist revolution, and—to a degree—of European imperialism as well; a patron of Ethiopia's Israeli ally; and, with the passage of the years, an advocate of conservative stability in the Horn, and even a reluctant opponent of Arab ambitions. The Americans were rich and powerful, and willing to help an old friend. After 1948, contacts bloomed. Ethiopian troops served with United Nations forces in Korea. In 1953, a Mutual Defense Agreement was signed; it was the most significant Ethiopian foreign policy decision of the generation. Between 1953 and 1970, Ethiopia received $147 million in military equipment, a huge amount for an African country and the foundation of the Ethiopian military establishment despite the Emperor's efforts to attract alternative support. At the time the original Agreement was signed, America in a separate accord received permission to establish a substantial radio-communications facility outside Asmara—Kagnew Station, named after the Ethiopian Brigade that fought in Korea. Kagnew cost $65 million and was originally manned by 1,500 specialists of the United States armed forces. The huge, electronic installation north of Asmara symbolizes a very real American presence in Ethiopia, one that provides crucial support for the Empire and some significant benefits for Washington as well.

But while Kagnew is convenient from Washington's point of view, it is not irreplaceable. Improvements in communications technology have reduced the facility's importance, and uncertainty about the stability of Eritrea prompted a search for an alternative. In December

1970, Washington announced plans to construct a radio-communications center on the island of Diego Garcia, south of India, a site without political complications. With Diego Garcia operational in 1973, the American presence at Kagnew is for the time being far more important to Ethiopia than to the United States, most specifically as a symbol of external support.

This support has been proffered to a nation whose international posture is bound to oppose America's major international rivals, Russia and China. No matter what regime rules in Addis Ababa, so long as the Amharic center holds, Ethiopia must look with suspicion on a Somalia backed by the Russians. Ethiopia, of course, has not limited its international ties. Indeed, the Emperor has made every effort to establish friendly relations with all countries. He has made trips to Eastern Europe and Russia, to China and the Arab states, and he has welcomed a whole spectrum of visiting dignitaries to his capital. But apart from the American connection, only the ties with France, because of Djibouti, and with Israel have assumed a significance much beyond ceremonial.

At the moment, there seems to be no pressure for change, no great American interest in reviewing ties with Ethiopia. The basic advantage to the United States is to create, at relatively little cost, a visible —but not too visible—American presence in an area of growing interest to the Soviets, perhaps even to China. This can most easily be done from Ethiopia. The old habits and suspicions almost guarantee that any Ethiopian regime will cling to the American connection. This means that in times of intra-Horn strife, American relations with Ethiopia's rivals will decay. There is little the United States can do to compete for the favor of the Somalis or Sudanese. Simply because of the American presence in Ethiopia, the Soviets found a built-in connection in Mogadishu. The fact that Washington has given help to Somalia in the past, has constructed a water-purifying plant, developed a fishery program, worked on port improvement, and sent Peace Corps volunteers, cannot compete with Russian military equipment, or even with its revolutionary rhetoric. And Washington has really not made the effort. In the Sudan, Russia's own inept policies destroyed Sudanese enthusiasm for the Socialist bloc and Socialist policies. The disappearance of the Russians was a net gain for Washington; but all that could then be done was to maintain friendly relations, and to encourage private investment in a period when the United States has little interest in foreign aid. So long as the Palestine problem exists and American "sponsorship" of Israel continues, then relations with Arab regimes—even African-Arab or Islamic-Somali regimes—will be troubled.

Russia

The Russians face somewhat the same problems in the Horn, but have fewer assets. Increasingly, as Russia has sought parity as a world power, Moscow has been willing to underwrite a variety of regimes for a variety of reasons. There has always been some Russian interest in the Horn, but not until the early 1960s were any visible overtures made. The Soviet Union then sent arms to the reactionary Imam of Yemen, and rebuilt the port of Hodeidah, in a triumph of pragmatism over ideology. The Soviet connection in South Arabia continued to grow with aid to the successor republic in San'a, and subsequently to the revolutionary regime in Aden. But the results have been mixed. After 1968, San'a grew conservative, depending on Saudi rather than Soviet subsidies, and Aden more radical, favoring the Chinese competitor. In the Sudan, after a decade of relatively moderate if ineffectual regimes, the Nimeiri coup in 1969 began an era of intensive collaboration with the Socialist bloc in general and Russia in particular. As a friend of the Arabs, before and after 1967, the Soviet Union hurried to aid the new regime—military advisors, equipment, naval visits, construction at Port Sudan. Simultaneously, the Soviets managed to commit a series of blunders, mainly economic arrangements solely to Russian advantage. The clumsy reaction to the attempted pro-Communist coup in 1971 was the finishing blow; Russia's prestige and position collapsed overnight.

In Somalia, the Russians found a more consistent ally. The first military assistance agreement, for $35 million in grants and credits, was signed in 1963. By the end of 1971, the total had grown to $50 million. There are now some 2,000 Soviet personnel in Somalia, including 300 military advisors. Perhaps up to 60 percent of the

Somali officer corps has been trained in Russia. Soviet economic assistance has waxed and waned; but after a visit by President Siad to Moscow in 1971, there has been renewed Soviet interest. Since the first grants, a total of $87 million in economic aid has been extended to date. A total of 1,500 Somali students had been brought to Russia for study by the end of 1972; 425 are still there. They may or may not be a Soviet asset; there is some evidence that the Somali government has chosen certain "students" mainly to get them out of the country.

Strategically, there are two interesting considerations. First, the Soviets are developing naval support facilities at the port of Berbera, including a military airport and two Soviet communications facilities that opened in December 1972. This should make possible a more comfortable peacetime naval deployment, and it may also be a harbinger for the future; but it is not yet a hard base. Second, the Somalis have declined to sign a friendship treaty with the Soviets similar to those Russia has negotiated with Egypt, Iran, and India. Somalia may be greatly dependent upon Russia, but is not yet a pawn. The Soviet connection has produced great concern in Addis Ababa, where Russia is regularly suspected of plotting against the regime. For the Ethiopians, there could be no more dangerous plot than to turn Somalia into a military threat, and Somalia now has the fifth largest army in Africa. This is Russia's doing.

The Soviet position in the Horn has thus varied a good deal. Russia crept into the Red Sea with the radical Arabs after the original agreements with Nasser. The creation of the Somali Republic in 1960, at a time of rising Soviet interest in the Third World, offered a logical opportunity to Moscow. Engaged in a confrontation with Ethiopia, the Somalis needed Soviet aid. Thus, the Soviets found a friend in what might someday become an important area. A year after the 1963 Somali Military Agreement, the Indian Ocean became potentially very important indeed to Soviet strategic interests. In 1964, the long-range United States Polaris A3 missile became operational, and thus transformed the Arabian Sea into a potential launching site. American submarines were not positioned in the Indian Ocean; but the prospect was not pleasing in Moscow, and provided the opportunity for the Russian naval establishment to urge a limited response. In 1968, the Soviet Navy entered the Indian Ocean. This naval presence should not be overstated. The Soviets have no permanent harbor facilities nor a supporting air arm; and lines of communication with home bases are long and thin.

But even if the Soviets were doing no more than picking up a minor option for future use, not—as alarmed Western observers suggested—shifting the whole balance of power, the naval visits underscored the potential of the Horn. As the naval tours continued, a pattern for the use of the Somali ports of Mogadishu, Berbera, and Kismayu developed. Between 1970 and 1971, there were 43 such calls. These visits do not imply at present a permanent Soviet naval presence, despite the construction of extensive oil storage facilities in Somali ports. Still, the Somalis—along with the regime in Aden across the Strait of Bab el-Mandeb—have become Russia's closest friends in the area. While it is possible that Russia would like more extensive facilities, a major Soviet naval deployment appears only as a future prospect. There can be no doubt, however, that Moscow feels the investment in the area—despite setbacks in Yemen and the Sudan—to be worth the time and trouble. Options are kept open, a strategic counterpresence to the Americans is maintained, the flag is shown, ideological allies given encouragement. Perhaps most important, parity with the other superpower is given visible form even in the Horn of Africa.

China

China is clearly not a major power in the Horn. Indeed, the Horn is a long way from China, and Peking has limited capital to invest outside the mainland. The significance of China lies in its capacity to cause serious instability with a relatively small investment. For many African regimes, Chinese involvement often proved either a threat or an embarrassment, or both. China became involved in supporting the ELF in Eritrea and in training Ethiopian rebel cadres. During the Cultural Revolution, many of these contacts withered as Peking withdrew into isolation. After the Nixon detente and the visible reemergence of the Chinese, Peking apparently no longer cared to be encumbered with these old ties, many with

highly inefficient revolutionaries. In the new atmosphere, Haile
Selassie himself undertook a state visit to Peking.

The present Chinese policy is to undertake development projects,
maintain a low profile, and keep a cheerful face. The political or
strategic purpose of these projects, funded out of limited resources,
is not clear. Competition with the Russians may produce a certain
momentum, as may the lure of ideology. The present posture, which
is tied to existing regimes and the needs of economic development,
could very well undergo another ideological change. No Sinologist
can be sure what the Chinese do want at this point—other than
to have friends everywhere and to keep an eye on the Russians; and
still less can they project Chinese intentions in the Horn over the
next decade. What is worrisome is that a quite decent revolution
can be purchased in the Horn for the price of a cotton mill; and there
could easily be another Cultural Revolution in China that might
favor subversion and exported revolution.

Israel and the Arabs

The Israelis and the Arabs are, on the other hand, quite scrutable
and their disagreements dangerous to the future stability of the
Horn. The Israelis have the most specific and exacting interests in
the area, not simply the desire to show the flag or to have access to a
port, but the pressing need for access to Asia through the Red Sea.
The difference between a blockade at Sharm-el-Shiekh at the top
of the Red Sea, and Bab el-Mandeb at the bottom, is only a matter
of distance, as the Israelis discovered in October 1973, during the
Yom Kippur War.

In the Horn, the Israelis found a ready-made ally in Ethiopia, a
nation tied by legend to the Biblical Hebrews, and more importantly,
a country imbued with an historical suspicion of Islam and the
Arabs. The Ethiopians felt the romantic ties of history more keenly
than the Israelis, but the pressing needs of the present made the
alliance obvious. An Israeli connection had advantages for Ethiopia
—training and arms from a friend, however small, other than the
United States, an ally that could be trusted and whose military

prowess was repeatedly confirmed. For Israel, a friendly Ethiopia permitted a watching brief on the two Straits and a position on the southern flank of the Arab world.

Israel used this position to harass the Sudan by aiding the rebels in the south. If the Khartoum government refused to treat with the rebels, Israeli aid would guarantee the continuation of the insurrection and the effective elimination of the Sudan from meaningful participation in Middle Eastern affairs. Ultimately, the Sudan had to chose between continued enfeeblement because of the drain of the southern war, or opting for an African solution that would also remove the country from the frontlines. Israel could hardly lose. In October 1973, however, the special relationship with Ethiopia came to an end when Addis Ababa, yielding to the pressures of African unity, with some reluctance severed diplomatic relations with Tel Aviv.

These harassing manuevers by one side or the other pose a grave danger to the Horn. Until 1967, Arab interest in the Horn had appeared to be declining. But for a variety of reasons, everything changed in that year. Nimeiri and Qaddaffi came to power. The British—and the Egyptians—left South Arabia. Israel arrived at the tip of Sinai and became a Red Sea power. And the Arabs could find no means to undo the events of June 1967. Frustrated along the cease-fire lines, the Arabs briefly placed some hope in the fedayeen, but then sought alternative means to wage the long war against Zionism. Qaddaffi in particular searched for an arena for confrontation with Zionists, with imperialists, with infidels. He aided Nimeiri as an Arab and opposed him as an African. He supported the ELF. He pointed out that the Israelis must be countered everywhere, even in the Horn.

Sporadic interest in the Red Sea continued in Cairo, where the pragmatic leadership knew the risks of challenging the Israelis. On October 27, 1972, *Al Ahram* suggested an Arab Naval Command in the Red Sea; but the project disappeared, came to nothing. Even without an open challenge, the very existence of the Arab-Israeli conflict has greatly raised the level of tension in the Horn. The

Black September assassinations in Khartoum forced unpleasant decisions on the Khartoum regime—to the delight, it is assumed, of Qaddaffi. Of all the great international issues, the Israeli-Arab confrontation is the most dangerous for the Horn. The great powers will manuever for advantage with the traditional weapons of diplomacy and development, military assistance and soft loans. The Arabs and Israelis are entangled in a more lethal confrontation, and could thus slip into open conflict at any point of contact—and contact has already been made at the southern end of the Red Sea and in the bush of the Sudan.

Others

Of the other major powers, only France with the responsibility for Djibouti has a political, and perhaps strategic, stake in the Horn, and only France of the former imperial powers in the area has a visible African policy to pursue. In a generation, the British presence has evaporated in the Sudan, Somalia, and Aden. The Italians have withdrawn from Somalia, and doubt the wisdom of their postcolonial investment there. Italians in Eritrea are regularly urged by Rome to return home. The new powers—whether the Japanese exploiting copper in Ethiopia, or the Bulgarians beginning a mining project in Las Koreh, Somalia—are not yet significant strategic factors. Japan may in time find that markets and economic projects in the Horn will involve more than simple economic considerations. But at the moment, only France with Djibouti is a serious factor.

This does not mean that other powers, independently or as surrogates, have no real interests in the Horn. Clearly the great shared interest, particularly in Europe, is the Horn's position along the Arabian oil-producing areas and abutting the oil routes. The demand for Arabian oil will increase massively over the next decade, and any renegade or revolutionary regime along the oil routes could cause untold trouble. Hence there is a general interest, particularly in Western Europe, in seeking stability in the Horn.

Conclusions

Internal Stability

Excluding the special case of Djibouti, the three principal states of the Horn face the same problems of development in traditional, conservative, rural societies prone to separatism and the pull of local loyalties. No regime can count heavily on undiscovered mineral wealth, which in each case may exist. All have to contend with an expanding population, urban immigration, rising popular expectations, and the resentments created by the unevenly bestowed benefits of modernization. All are heavily dependent on distant commodity markets, distant money markets, and on the future economic priorities of distant patrons. To exploit potential agricultural wealth—transforming unused or underused land into productive areas, creating the infrastructure to sort, move, and sell the goods, and then reinvesting the returns wisely for future development—are tremendous challenges for all of those regimes, given the existing and potential availability of trained personnel. Yet a rational and effective agricultural policy is the foundation for all future progress and stability.

Given the competing priorities, limited resources, and the heritage of the past, the prospects for smooth progress toward a modern society are not good. No one believes that all Ethiopians will be functionally literate by the year 2000, or that the southern Sudan will be transformed into a new Garden of Eden. Even to run in place has become an awesome challenge. All of these countries,

47

whatever their ideological posture or development strategy, face
internal discontent, severe economic and social pressures, and perhaps armed opposition. They would have problems beyond their
immediate capacity to solve even without the existence of regional
strains.

Regional Strains

For the Horn, 1972 was a good year, during which the forces of
reason and stability swept the board. The March 1972 agreement
that ended the long rebellion in the southern Sudan, followed by the
Ethiopian-Sudanese border agreement, the emergence of Nimeiri as
a major African figure, the new-formed "maturity" of the government in Mogadishu were all encouraging developments. For five
years, there had been little agitation for a Greater Somalia; and
for two years there, had been a decline in ELF activity in Eritrea.
By 1973, the Horn was enjoying a rare state of equilibrium; and
the immediate prospects appeared equally promising.

At any point, however, this stability could be challenged by old
quarrels, the lures of personal ambition, by accident or malice or the
need for foreign adventure. Greater Somalia was not dead. When
Mogadishu raised the issue at the May 1973 session of the AOU,
the old, divisive wrangling began again. The ELF has not given up
hope in the area. As for the Sudan, some future officer may prefer
to serve as President of a rebel republic of the upper Nile than as
a minor minister in Khartoum. An abrupt change in Djibouti would
surely rupture Ethiopian-Somali relations. A militant revival of
Islam or a revolutionary plot could well cross boundaries and
rekindle ancient quarrels. Even during an era of stability, the old
ambitions and suspicions will only gradually erode.

International Pressures

The fact that two major international confrontations cut across
the Horn, geographically and ideologically, guarantees a certain

level of tension at the best of times. While it is true that the East-West face-off has been muted, and complicated, by the Nixon policy of detente, the strategic interests of East and West in the Horn of Africa are hardly complementary. The prospect of an escalating Chinese-Russian rivalry in the Horn is also not unlikely. The Israeli-Arab conflict always threatens to erupt again, and any prospect of a permanent accommodation seems faint. At any time, the Arabs could trigger a new war, as they did in the Fall 1973 Yom Kippur War. Added to all this is the old cutting edge of Islam, newly honed in Libya. Qaddaffi's efforts to win allies across the African board, to aid Islamic causes, and to punish enemies of the faith can only aggravate tension along Africa's Black-and-Tan fault, a fault that cuts through the Horn. Even the beneficial effects of African nationalism and unity oppose the interests of Islam as defined by Qaddaffi.

Strategic Implications

The immediate strategic interests of the powers vary. For Israel, they are vital; for France, marginal; for Italy, nearly nonexistent. What is more important, the Horn does have strategic value for those powers with world pretensions, and the complexity of weapons technology may well increase that value during the next decade. While analysis of long-term Soviet or American strategic needs, the future significance of seapower in the Indian Ocean, or the ultimate impact of any SALT agreements is crucial, two things become clear when these factors are linked with the Horn. First, the Horn's particular importance is geographical. Since it is likely that the Indian Ocean, the Red Sea, and the main oil routes will become more, not less, important in the period ahead, the Horn's importance will also increase. Second, any exploitation of these geographical assets depends on conditions within the Horn, conditions structured by regional geography, ethnic rivalry, and historical attitudes.

Bibliography

There are no recent nor readily available treatments of the strategic implications of the Horn; in fact, the region is rarely treated as a unit, nor have the specific interests of individual powers been examined in much detail. Although not directed toward the Horn alone, Geoffrey Jukes, *The Indian Ocean in Soviet Naval Policy*, Adelphi Paper 87 (London: International Institute for Strategic Studies, 1972) is valuable, as is the annual *Military Balance* (London: International Institute for Strategic Studies). Those interested in the contemporary Horn must rely on journals like *New Middle East*, *Jeune Afrique*, special reports like *Africa Confidential* (London) or the occasional academic article, such as J. Bowyer Bell, "Bab el-Mandeb, Strategic Troublespot," *Orbis*, vol. 16, no. 4 (Winter 1973).

Ethiopia

Clapham, Christopher, *Haile Selassie's Government* (New York: Praeger, 1969).
———. "Imperial Leadership in Ethiopia," *African Affairs*, vol. 68 (1968).
Greenfield, Richard. *Ethiopia, A New Political History* (New York: Praeger, 1965).
Halliday, Fred. "The Fighting in Eritrea," *New Left Review*, no. 67 (May-June 1971).

Hess, Robert L. *Ethiopia, The Modernization of Autocracy* (Ithaca: Cornell University Press, 1970).
Jones, A. H. M., and Monroe, Elizabeth. *A History of Ethiopia* (Oxford: Clarendon Press, 1960).
Perham, Margery. *The Government of Ethiopia* (London: Faber and Faber, 1969).
Taylor, Graham. "Rebellion in Eritrea," *New Middle East,* no. 31 (April 1971).
United States Army Handbook for Ethiopia. (Washington: US Government Printing Office, 1964).
Yakobson, S. "Soviet Union and Ethiopia: A Case of Traditional Behavior," *Review of Politics,* vol. 25 (July 1963).

Somalia

Drysdale, John. *The Somalia Dispute* (London: Pall Mall, 1964).
Hoskyns, Catherine. *Case Studies in African Diplomacy: The Ethiopi-Somali-Kenya Dispute 1960-1967* (Dar-es-Salaam: Oxford University Press for Institute of Public Administration, University College, 1969).
Lewis, I.M. *The Modern History of Somaliland* (London: Weidenfeld and Nicolson, 1965).
—————. *Pastoral Democracy* (London: Oxford University Press, 1961).
Touval, Saadia. *Somali Nationalism* (Cambridge: Harvard University Press, 1963).

Djibouti

Thompson, Virginia, and Adloff, Richard. *Djibouti and the Horn of Africa* (Stanford: Stanford University Press, 1968).

Sudan

Albino, Oliver. *The Sudan, A Southern Viewpoint* (London: Oxford University Press, 1970).

Bell, J. Bowyer. "The Sudan's New African Policy, Problems and Prospects," *Africa Today* (Sumner 1973).

Beshir, Mohamed Omer. *The Southern Sudan, Background to Conflict* (London: Hurst, 1968).

First, Ruth. *Power in Africa* (New York: Pantheon, 1970).

Holt, P. M. *A Modern History of the Sudan* (London: Weidenfeld and Nicolson, 1961).

El-Mahdi, Mandour. *A Short History of the Sudan* (London: Oxford University Press, 1965).

Mazrui, Ali A. "The Multiple Marginality of the Sudan," in *Sudan in Africa* (Khartoum: Khartoum University Press, 1971).

National Strategy Information Center, Inc.

Strategy Papers

Edited by Frank N. Trager and William Henderson
With the assistance of Dorothy E. Nicolosi

The Horn of Africa by J. Bowyer Bell, Jr., December 1973

Research and Development and the Prospects for International Security by Frederick Seitz and Rodney W. Nichols, December 1973

Raw Material Supply in a Multipolar World by Yuan-li Wu, October 1973

The People's Liberation Army: Communist China's Armed Forces by Angus M. Fraser, August 1973

Nuclear Weapons and the Atlantic Alliance by Wynfred Joshua, May 1973

How to Think About Arms Control and Disarmament by James E. Dougherty, May 1973

The Military Indoctrination of Soviet Youth by Leon Gouré, January 1973

The Asian Alliance: Japan and United States Policy by Franz Michael and Gaston J. Sigur, October 1972

Iran, The Arabian Peninsula, and the Indian Ocean by R. M. Burrell and Alvin J. Cottrell, September 1972

Soviet Naval Power: Challenge for the 1970s by Norman Polmar, April 1972

How Can We Negotiate with the Communists? by Gerald L. Steibel, March 1972

Soviet Political Warfare Techniques, Espionage and Propaganda in the 1970s by Lyman B. Kirkpatrick, Jr., and Howland H. Sargeant, January 1972

The Soviet Presence in the Eastern Mediterranean by Lawrence L. Whitten, September 1971

The Military Unbalance
Is the U.S. Becoming a Second-Class Power? June 1971

The Future of South Vietnam by Brigadier F. P. Serong, February 1971 (Out of print)

Strategy and National Interests: Reflections for the Future by Bernard Brodie, January 1971

The Mekong River: A Challenge in Peaceful Development for Southeast Asia by Eugene R. Black, December 1970

Problems of Strategy in the Pacific and Indian Oceans by George G. Thomson, October 1970

Soviet Penetration into the Middle East by Wynfred Joshua, July 1970. Revised edition, October 1971

Australian Security Policies and Problems by Justus M. van der Kroef, May 1970

Detente: Dilemma or Disaster? by Gerald L. Steibel, July 1969

The Prudent Case for Safeguard by William R. Kintner, June 1969

Forthcoming

The Soviet Presence in Latin America by James D. Theberge

The Development of Strategic Weapons by Norman Polmar

Contemporary Soviet Defense Policy by Benjamin S. Lambeth

NATIONAL STRATEGY INFORMATION CENTER, INC.